Growing Things

The World's Largest Plants

A Book About Trees

Written by Susan Blackaby

Illustrated by Charlene DeLage

Content Adviser: Jeffrey H. Gillman, Ph.D., Assistant Professor
Horticultural Science, University of Minnesota, St. Paul, Minnesota

Reading Adviser: Susan Kesselring, M.A., Literacy Educator
Rosemount-Apple Valley-Eagan (Minnesota) School District

PICTURE WINDOW BOOKS
Minneapolis, Minnesota

Editor: Nadia Higgins
Designer: Nathan Gassman
Page production: Picture Window Books
The illustrations in this book were painted with watercolor.

Picture Window Books
5115 Excelsior Boulevard
Suite 232
Minneapolis, MN 55416
1-877-845-8392
www.picturewindowbooks.com

Printed in the United States of America.
1 2 3 4 5 6 08 07 06 05 04 03

Library of Congress Cataloging-in-Publication Data
Blackaby, Susan.
The world's largest plants : a book about trees / written by Susan Blackaby ; illustrated by Charlene DeLage.
v. cm. — (Growing things)
Contents: What is a tree?—Types of trees—Making and storing food—Parts of the stem—
Depending on trees—Bark rubbings—Fun facts—Comparing trees.
ISBN 1-4048-0110-3 (Library Binding)
1. Trees—Juvenile literature. [1. Trees.] I. DeLage, Charlene, 1944-ill. II. Title.
QK475.8 .B58 2003
582.16—dc21
2002156589

What Is a Tree?

Plants come in all sizes, from very small to very big.

The very biggest plants are trees.

Table of Contents

A tree is a plant with just one main, woody stem.
The woody stem is the trunk.

A young tree is called a sapling. Saplings grow tall and spread wide.

They become trees. Being tall helps trees reach the sunlight they need to make food.

Types of Trees

There are two main kinds of trees. One kind is a broad-leaved tree. Its leaves are thin and flat. Broad-leaved trees can be shaped like globes or eggs or umbrellas.

Where winters are cold, most broad-leaved trees lose their leaves.
In the fall, the leaves turn yellow, gold, red, orange, and brown.
When the temperature drops, so do the leaves.

Some broad-leaved
trees you know:
Maple
Oak
Birch
Apple
Cherry

9

The other kind of tree is called a conifer. Many conifers have needles instead of leaves. Some conifers have a triangle shape. That helps snow slide off the branches.

Conifers have cones. Most conifers are evergreens.
An evergreen stays green all year.

Some conifers you know:
Fir
Cedar
Spruce
Pine

Making and Storing Food

Like other plants, trees spend the summer making food. The roots soak up nutrients and water from the ground. The green parts soak up sunlight and air.

The food the tree makes is called sap.

Sap is stored in the trunk over the winter.

The tree uses the stored sap to grow new leaves in the spring.

Parts of the Stem

A tree trunk has a solid core of strong wood.
It is called heartwood. It holds up the tree.

Around the heartwood is a layer of sapwood.

The sapwood carries the water and nutrients from the roots up to the leaves.

Around the sapwood is a layer of inner bark.

The inner bark carries food from the leaves down to the roots.

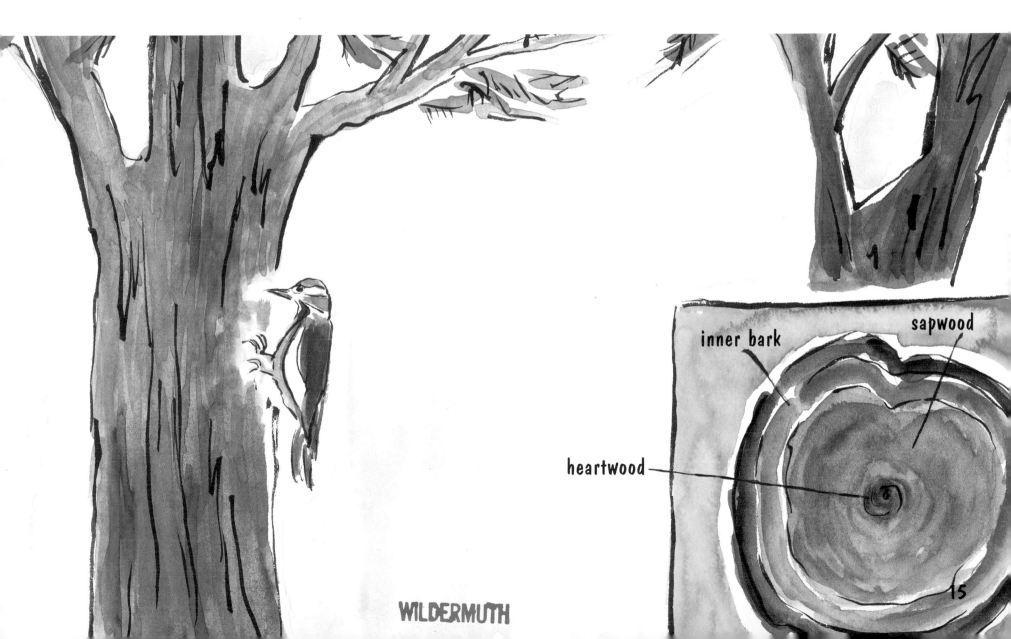

inner bark

sapwood

heartwood

WILDERMUTH

15

A tough layer of bark protects the outside of the tree. The bark keeps insects out and water in. If the bark is cut, sticky goo called pitch oozes out to seal up the hole.

Older trees have thick, rough bark. Saplings have smooth, thin bark.
As the tree grows bigger, the outer bark splits and breaks off.
New bark takes the place of the old bark.

Each year, a new layer of wood grows below the bark.
The layer makes a ring around the whole tree.

Each ring has two colors.

The light part is called early wood because it grows in the spring.

The dark part is called late wood because it grows in the summer.

Tree rings can tell us a lot of things about the past. Counting tree rings can tell how old the tree is. Some years, the ring is thick. It can show a rainy spring or a cool summer. Some years, the ring is thin. It can show a dry year. Some years, the ring is scarred. It can show a year with a bad fire or a lot of hungry insects.

19

Depending on Trees

Trees help people and the planet in many ways. Trees give us wood to build homes. Trees give us fuel to keep us warm. In summer, they make cool shade.

Trees give us fruit and nuts to eat. They give us oxygen to breathe.
Trees make our planet a green and healthy place.

Bark Rubbings

Bark can be smooth, rough, papery, or scaly.
It can peel off in little sheets or break off in chunks.
It can be hard or spongy.
It can be green, gold, white, red, gray, silver, brown, or black.
Study bark by taking rubbings.
Hold a sheet of paper against a tree trunk.
Rub the side of a crayon over the sheet.
Keep rubbing until the bark pattern appears.
How many different kinds of bark patterns can you find?

Fun Facts

- The ginkgo tree is the oldest tree on the planet.
  Leaves from ginkgoes were munched by dinosaurs!
- Native Americans made lightweight canoes
  out of bark. They carved heavy dugout canoes out
  of tree trunks.
- Rubber is made of gummy sap from the rubber tree.
- Maple syrup is made from the sweet sap
  of the maple tree.
- Paper is made from a mix of chopped up wood and
  water. It is poured out, pressed, and then dried
  to make sheets.
- Broad-leaved trees are evergreen in tropical places,
  where it is warm and rainy all year.

Comparing Trees

This diagram compares conifers to broad-leaved trees. How are they alike? How are they different?

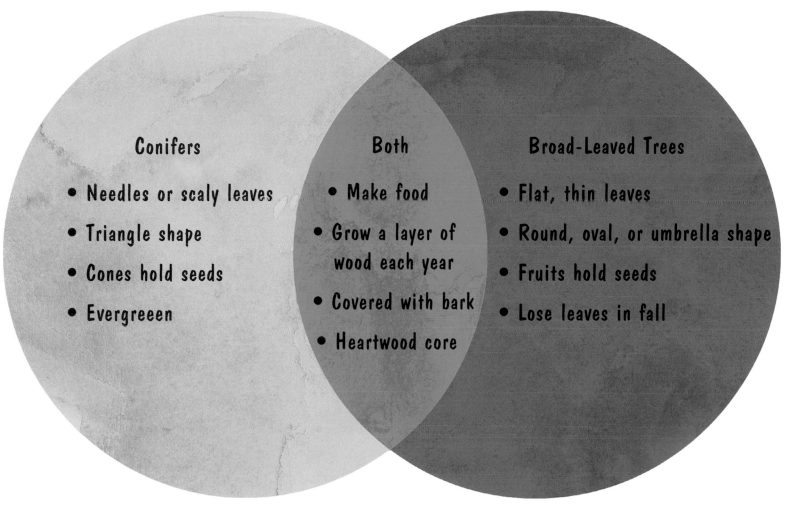

Conifers

- Needles or scaly leaves
- Triangle shape
- Cones hold seeds
- Evergreeen

Both

- Make food
- Grow a layer of wood each year
- Covered with bark
- Heartwood core

Broad-Leaved Trees

- Flat, thin leaves
- Round, oval, or umbrella shape
- Fruits hold seeds
- Lose leaves in fall

Words to Know

broad-leaved tree—a tree with thin, flat leaves instead of needles
conifer—a tree with cones instead of flowers
evergreen—a plant that stays green all year round
nutrients—parts of food, like vitamins, that are used for growth
sap—food that the tree makes and stores for growth
sapling—a young tree

To Learn More

At the Library

Gibbons, Gail. *Tell Me, Tree: All About Trees for Kids.* Boston: Little, Brown & Co.: 2002.
Lauber, Patricia. *Be a Friend to Trees.* New York: HarperCollins, 1994.
Vieira, Linda. *The Ever-Living Tree: The Life and Times of a Coast Redwood.* New York: Walker, 1994.

On the Web

EPA Kids' Site
http://www.epa.gov/kids
For information about exploring and protecting nature

Redwood National and State Parks Kids' Page
http://www.nps.gov/redw/kids.html
For fun facts and activities on Redwood National and State Parks

Want more information about trees? FACT HOUND offers a safe, fun way to find Web sites. All of the sites on Fact Hound have been researched by our staff.
Simply follow these steps:

1. Visit *http://www.facthound.com.*
2. Enter a search word or 1404801103.
3. Click Fetch It.

Your trusty Fact Hound will fetch the best sites for you!

Index